Successful
Time
Management
in a week

Declan Treacy

Headway · Hodder & Stoughton

2003064 548

British Library Cataloguing in Publication Data

Treacy, Declan
Successful Time Management in a Week. –
(Successful Business in a Week Series)
I. Title II. Series

ISBN 0 340 58763 6   658.4093

First published 1993
Impression number   10   9   8   7   6   5   4   3   2
Year   1998   1997   1996   1995   1994   1993

Typeset by Multiplex Techniques Ltd, St Mary Cray, Kent.
Printed for Hodder & Stoughton Educational, a division of
Hodder Headline Plc, Mill Road, Dunton Green, Sevenoaks,
Kent by Colorcraft Ltd.

the Institute
of Management

F O U N D A T I O N

The Institute of Management (IM) is at the forefront of management development and best management practice. The Institute embraces all levels of management from students to chief executives. It provides a unique portfolio of services for all managers, enabling them to develop skills and achieve management excellence.

For information on the benefits of membership, please write to:

Department HS
Institute of Management
Cottingham Road
Corby
Northants NN17 1TT

This series is commissioned by the Institute of Management Foundation.

C O N T E N T S

It's been a hectic day as usual. The phone has rung at least a dozen times, I've attended three meetings, I couldn't begin to count the pieces of paper I've handled, I've dealt with five queries from colleagues who unexpectedly arrived in my office, and there have been two major crises to sort out. I've been so busy but, you know, I don't really feel as if I have achieved anything.

Many of us recognise the feelings expressed by the manager above. We work hard but there seems to be too much to do and just not enough time.

There are 86,400 seconds in each day. Why is it that some people can run large organisations or even countries within that time while others seem to get bogged down in the simplest of jobs? The secret lies in effective time management.

Over the next week we are going to fine tune our time management skills step by step. Each day, we will explore a new topic and after reviewing the theory, the checklists and exercises will encourage us to apply the principles to our own work situation. All the time management techniques recommended in this book are already being practised by successful managers. We only have to look around to see.

Our agenda for the week is as follows:

Sunday	– Self-assessment
Monday	– Mastering paperwork
Tuesday	– Planning
Wednesday	– Managing meetings
Thursday	– Managing projects
Friday	– Taming the telephone
Saturday	– Review and additional time tips

To get the most out of this book, we will need to set aside one hour a day to work through it. Approximately 45 minutes should be spent reviewing each chapter and completing the exercises, and 15 minutes reviewing our performance at the end of each day. We should start as we mean to go on by blocking off these time periods in our diary now!

For many of its readers, this book will serve as a catalyst for a dramatic change in their working lives; for others, it will serve only to pass a few hours with little real benefit. Only we can determine which category we will fit into. If we choose to change, the benefits of good time management are immediate and substantial. We will:

- Achieve better results
- Improve the quality of our work
- Work faster
- Lower our stress levels
- Make fewer mistakes
- Reduce the number of crises faced
- Increase our salary
- Improve our work satisfaction
- Improve the quality of our non-working life

Remember: *it is what we do during the 86,400 seconds of each day that will ultimately determine how successful we are in our chosen career.*

Office Productivity Week

Office Productivity Week takes place during the first week of September every year. We should set aside this week, or another more appropriate one, to get everyone else in the office organised. As managers we are responsible for the performance of the people around us. If one of our colleagues is buried under a mountain of paperwork the chaos will have a negative effect upon the rest of the office. If someone else consistently fails to plan their projects, everyone else will suffer when the ensuing crises materialise. Everyone in our department and throughout the company should be encouraged to take part.

Each day of Office Productivity Week should be devoted to a different aspect of time management, ideally following the agenda on p.6. At least one hour of the day should be set aside for a group discussion on the topic of the day. A copy of this book should be distributed to everyone taking part beforehand so that they can complete the exercises, and commit themselves to becoming better organised. With everyone involved, potential conflicts can be brought out into the open, and a consensus about how to tackle problems can be achieved.

At the end of each day, as we go through this book, we will look at some of the things that should be done during these group discussions to improve the time management skills of our colleagues.

Office Productivity Week seminars

Declan Treacy runs in-company seminars which follow the
outline of Office Productivity Week. On Monday,
participants will discover how to master their paperwork;
on Tuesday they will unlock the secrets of successful
planning etc. Everyone taking part attends a one-hour
session each day of the week. To keep groups down to a
manageable size, up to six sessions can be held on each day.
This ensures that if people cannot attend a session at the
same time every day they have five other sessions to choose
from.

Each participant is asked to complete a number of exercises
beforehand in order to benefit fully from the session. After
reviewing the theory they will be divided into smaller groups
and asked to come up with action steps they will follow when
they go back to the office. With everyone in a department or
company involved in these sessions there is a group motivation
to become more productive. If one person slips back into old
habits a week after the seminar, other members of the group
can bring them back onto the right track.

The sessions are highly participative. For example, on the Monday, which is managing paperwork day, each individual is asked to bring along all the unnecessary paper that has landed on their desk during the previous week. Part of the session will be set aside to work through this stack of papers, with the group being asked to decide how to prevent this paperwork being generated in future. On Wednesday (meetings day), half of the group will be asked to hold a 10 minute meeting on a particular topic while the other half observes. Each person taking part in the meeting will be rated according to the management checklists for meetings. The mini-meeting will also be videotaped and run back to isolate effective and unproductive contributions to the meeting. The role-play theme will be continued on other days of the week.

A one-hour follow-up session is scheduled two weeks later, during which individuals can discuss their progress and sort out any unresolved problems.

The address from which further details on Office Productivity Week and the seminars can be obtained is given at the back of the book.

Self-assessment

Today, we are going to evaluate our current time management skills. This is a very important exercise and will form the foundation of our future success. By the end of today, we will have completed a time log, made a list of our top 10 timewasters and explored the process by which we will develop timesaving habits.

Self-assessment
- Analysing our current use of time
- Identifying the timewasters
- Changing our habits

Analysing our current use of time

The first step in improving our time management skills is to analyse how we currently spend our time. Research has shown that managers constantly need to change the focus of their attention, and spend an average of only 10 minutes on each task throughout the day. We can easily get swept along in the cut and thrust of daily office life without appreciating where our time goes.

In this section we will complete a self-assessment questionnaire and compile a time log. Both exercises give us the opportunity to stand back and evaluate our performance objectively. A special notebook should be obtained and used for these exercise and all others in the book.

The self-assessment questionnaire:

	Yes	No
I tend not to tackle paperwork the first time I see it	☐	☐
I face more crises than I need to because of poor planning	☐	☐
I sometimes have to be chased by others to get things done	☐	☐
I have a vague idea of what my priorities are	☐	☐
I spend more than 30 minutes a day looking for things	☐	☐
My meetings tend to last longer than necessary	☐	☐
I allow others to negatively influence how I spend my time	☐	☐
I start a lot more projects than I finish	☐	☐
I am always busy but not always productive	☐	☐
I hang on to tasks that should really be delegated	☐	☐

If we have answered 'Yes' to five or more of the statements above then the week ahead will provide us with some much needed insights and solutions to our time management problems. Regardless of our score we should come back to the questionnaire at the end of the week and complete it again.

Compiling a time log will provide us with some additional insights. A time log as shown overleaf should be made up and completed for Thursday and Friday of last week. Each task completed during the day should be written down, along with an estimate of its duration: telephone calls, correspondence, meetings, interruptions, memos, junk mail and so on. We should note down whether the task was planned or not, and then estimate its pay-off. This exercise might also be carried out on Monday and Tuesday of this week to give us a further insight into our time management, and then periodically every few months to gauge our improvement.

Time log

Time	Activity	Pay-off	Duration	Planned
9.00	coffee/chatted with colleagues	low	15 mins	no
9.15	processed mail	med	25 mins	yes
9.40	sales call	low	5 mins	no
9.45	fax arrived	high	20 mins	no
10.05	follow-up call	high	10 mins	no
10.15	colleague dropped by to talk about contract	med	15 mins	no
10.30	sales meeting	med	85 mins	yes
11.55	dealt with telephone messages	med	20 mins	no
12.15	browsed through leaflets left in in-tray	low	10 mins	no
:	:	:	:	:
:	:	:	:	:
:	:	:	:	:
:	:	:	:	:
4.00	draft report for MD	high	70 mins	yes

After completing the time log we should ask ourselves the following questions:

- What proportion of my tasks were planned?
- Was there any real structure to my day?
- Did planned tasks take longer than expected?
- Why did I spend so long on the low pay-off tasks?
- How many interruptions did I face?
- During what part of the day was I most productive?
- Have I been productive, or just busy?
- What can I do to gain greater control over my time?
- What proportion of my time could I realistically plan for?
- On a scale of 1-10 how would I rate my effectiveness?

Identifying the timewasters

When completing a time log, many people are shocked at the amount of time that is wasted during the day. People we don't need to talk to are on the phone, colleagues are constantly dropping by for a chat, bits of paper are mislaid, meetings last longer than expected. Our days seem to be saturated with timewasters: low pay-off activities that deflect us from the important work .

The list overleaf outlines the 10 most common timewasters. After considering each item on the list we should compile a list of our own top 10 timewasters.

The 10 most common timewasters

1   Losing things
2   Meetings
3   Telephone
4   Interruptions
5   Procrastination
6   Junk paperwork
7   Crises
8   Reverse delegation
9   Perfectionism
10 Distractions

Let's look at these timewasters in more detail.

Losing things

How much time is spent rummaging amongst the pile of
papers on the desk in the typical week? If we spend just 30
seconds every five minutes extracting an item from the
bottom of the in-tray, looking for a telephone number we
scribbled down on a loose piece of paper, or locating a
misfiled document, it adds up to four hours a week. Time
we can't really afford to waste. How often do we have to do
things twice because we lost the original?

Meetings

How much of our time is spent in meetings every week?
What proportion of that time is wasted due to meetings that
should never have been held in the first place? How much
time do we waste because meetings start late or overrun? Do

we often have to sit through long meetings and find that only five minutes are relevant to us ?

Telephone
How many times does the telephone ring every day? What proportion of these calls are unexpected? What is the average length of each call? What proportion of these calls are really necessary? Do we allow our calls to drag on for longer than they should? Do we ever find ourselves ringing someone back because there was something we forgot to discuss during the first call?

Interruptions
How many times a day are we interrupted by colleagues arriving at the desk? Are these interruptions really necessary? Do these interruptions have a negative effect on our performance? Do we encourage social interruptions by always stopping what we are doing and chatting to people?

Procrastination

What tasks have we been avoiding over the past few weeks?
What excuses have been used to delay action? What is
usually the end result of our procrastination?

Junk paperwork

Are we as ruthless as we should be about getting rid of junk
mail? Do we resist delegating certain tasks because we enjoy
doing them? Do we find ourselves browsing through
magazines, newsletters and brochures when there is higher
pay-off work to be done?

Crises

Do we spend our days spent rushing around dealing with
one crisis after another? Is every crisis we deal with really a
crisis? Is every crisis that we deal with really our problem? If
we were more pro-active would we have avoided some of
these crises?

Reverse delegation

Do we respond to requests for help by saying, 'leave it with me, I'll tackle it later?'. Is there work on the desk that our subordinates have left for our input?

Perfectionism

Do we spend extra time getting things 100% right when 95% would do? Does our attention to detail on one project mean that something else more important doesn't get done?

Distractions

In the middle of one task, do we often find our attention being grabbed by other work around us on the desk? How do these distractions affect our workflow?

Working through our own personal list of timewasters, we should ask ourselves how much time we waste in each category during the typical week.

Telephone	48 mins
Crisis management	45 mins
Meetings	25 mins
Interruptions	19 mins
:	:
:	:
:	:
:	:
Distractions	7 mins

Changing our habits

The identification of our timewasters has been a major step
forward. We now need to concentrate on eliminating those
timewasting habits and substituting timesaving habits in
their place.

Many of these timewasters will have become a natural part
of our work style: allowing meetings to drag on, retaining
junk mail, procrastination. The first time we organised a
meeting that was running over time we probably looked
impatiently at our watch and shuffled our papers but
decided to say nothing. The next time it happened, we
might have noted that the meeting was running late, again
without commenting. Day after day, week after week, we
allowed our meetings to overrun. The timewasting
behaviour was repeated so often that it gradually became an
unconscious habit. Now our meetings don't finish until
everyone has stopped talking. We expect them to drag on
and therefore don't even set a finishing time when
arranging them.

Now is the time to change; to reverse the process.

Reading this book alone will not help us to alter our timewasting habits; it will take time and effort. If we were learning to play a musical instrument we would not be able to read a book and step straight on to the concert platform to give a virtuoso performance. The psychologists say it takes approximately 21 days to change a work habit. At first, we will have to make a conscious effort to keep our meetings on track and if things are dragging on, we need to stand up and indicate that the meeting is over. It will of course be difficult at first but once we have done it a few times it will become easier. From time to time, we will lapse back into our old habits, but perseverance will bring rewards in the long run. The decision to change is ours alone and the best time to change is now! Twenty years from now, many of this book's readers will be attending seminars and buying books on managing meetings.

The four-step process of change
The four-step process below should be applied to each of our timewasters. Procrastination will be used as an example.

If procrastination is one of our major timewasters, we probably put off things using excuses such as, 'I'm too busy right now', 'I need to wait for more information', or 'I'll do it tomorrow'. We might start off at the beginning of the day by pushing aside just one item, but it is soon joined by other documents. As more and more unfinished papers join the pile at the bottom of the action tray, we resist approaching that part of the desk. If we tackle one item, we will have to face everything, causing an immediate flood of guilt and stress. Subconsciously, we say to ourselves, 'Now what can I do instead ?'.

1   Write down the timewaster
On the top of a new page in our time management notebook
we should write down the timewaster: Procrastination.

2   List the problems caused by the timewasting habit
Next we need to list the problems faced as a result of
procrastination: constantly feeling guilty about unfinished
work, increased stress levels, spending too much time on the
enjoyable things which bring few rewards, a reputation
around the office as someone who is unreliable.

3   Visualise the timesaving habit
All thoughts of procrastination should be removed from our
minds and we should visualise ourselves as 'doers'. What
would things be like in the office if we had the reputation
for getting things done, rather than for procrastinating?
How would we handle our correspondence? How would
we approach difficult reports? How much unfinished work
would there be lying in the in-tray? The benefits of being a
'doer' should be written down.

4 Develop the timesaving habit

Next we need to write down the steps that are necessary to change our timewasting habit:

a I will stop using phoney excuses like, 'I need to wait for more information';

b I will have to remove tempting distractions such as brochures and magazines from my line of sight;

c I need to spend more time planning my day;

d I need to break down large projects into more manageable tasks;

e I will finish the uncomfortable items first and then reward myself with more enjoyable tasks.

This four-step process should be followed for each of our top 10 timewasters. One page in our time management notebook should be devoted to each timewaster: listing the problems it causes, visualising the way we want things to be in future and writing down the steps we need to take to change our timewaster to a timesaver. Every day during the the coming week, a few minutes should be spent reviewing our notebook to remind ourselves of the things that need to change.

Group time management exercises

Each member of the group should work through the exercises in this chapter: the self-assessment questionnaire, the time log and the timewasters exercise. A one-hour meeting should then be held during which each individual should stand up and identify their time management strengths and weaknesses. Once feedback has been received from the group, each person should identify the three timewasting habits they intend to eliminate over the coming weeks and months. Each person should be assigned a partner who will help them to improve their time management skills over the coming weeks and months. This mutual support system will ease the difficult journey ahead.

Tomorrow, we will focus on conquering the paper mountain. We cannot begin to manage our time effectively until we have gained control of the paper flow.

Mastering paperwork

Despite predictions about the move towards the paperless office, we still seem to be drowning in a sea of paper, much of it unnecessary. Today, we are going to look at ways of controlling the constant flow of paperwork arriving on the desk. By the end of the day, the desk will be clear of paperwork, we will have implemented techniques for reducing the inflow of unnecessary paperwork, and we will have streamlined and reorganised our files. This is necessary because it is essential to create the right physical environment before we can begin to manage our time effectively.

Mastering paperwork

- Paperwork reduction campaign
- Effective paper handling
- Effective filing

Paperwork reduction campaign

It is only by eliminating the low pay-off items that we can be free to concentrate on the important paperwork. If we examine all the memos, reports, faxes, letters, magazines, invoices, junk mail and other bits of paper that arrive on a daily basis, it becomes clear that most of it should never have been generated in the first place.

We frequently blame others for our paperwork problems, but it is often our own work style that causes the heavy inflow of paper. How often can we be heard to say to

colleagues, 'Send me a copy for my files', 'Could you confirm that in writing?', 'Write me a report on it', 'Send a memo around to everyone', or 'I can't act on that unless I have it in writing'? Before asking others to send paperwork, we should ask ourselves if the information is really necessary. If we need the information, we should try to obtain it by word of mouth or through the computer. Paper should be our last resort. We also complain about the amount of junk mail we receive but then deal with unwanted telesales callers by saying, 'Send me some information'.

As well as reducing the inflow of paperwork, we need to cut down the outflow from the desk. If we are constantly distributing forms, memos and photocopies to others, we can expect nothing less than an avalanche of paperwork in return. We should spend 30 minutes today devising and implementing strategies for reducing paperwork. The checklist below serves as a useful starting point.

> *Paperwork reduction checklist*
>
> - Have name removed from external mailing lists
> - Remove name from internal circulation lists
> - Ask colleagues to be concise
> - Where necessary have paperwork rerouted
> - Talk to people instead of writing
> - Ask colleagues to report by exception
> - Reduce the volume of paperwork leaving the desk
> - Return unnecessary paperwork to sender

We should set a definite target for reducing paper in the office over the next few months and enlist the help of our colleagues. Less paper means lower costs, improved productivity, improved morale, improved communications and a better service for our customers.

Effective paper handling

Ideally, each piece of paper that arrives on the desk should be handled only once. Few of us can afford the luxury of picking up the same piece of paper again and again without actioning it. If we are handling the same bits of paper over and over again we will be extremely busy but at the end of the day we will not have actually achieved anything extra.

The measles test
An exercise that will encourage us to handle paperwork the first time we see it is the measles test. For the next week, every time we pick up a piece of paper to deal with it, we should use a red marker and place a red dot on the page. If by the end of the week most of the paperwork on the desk

has had an outbreak of measles, then we know we need to change our habits.

The lack of a system for processing incoming paperwork, combined with our natural tendency to be indecisive, results in stacks of unfinished paperwork building up on the desk. Many of us work in chaotic environments and rationalise it with statements such as, 'I know where everything is!', 'It suits my personality!' or 'It's organised chaos!'.

We can always find an excuse, but research and common sense tells us that the chaotic desk leads to:

- Low productivity
- Missed opportunities and deadlines
- Frantic searches for lost information
- Long working hours
- High stress levels
- Low morale
- Unwanted distractions
- Unexpected crises

Working through the list above, we should try to recall the things that have gone wrong in our office in the past week because of paperwork mismanagement.

Before we can begin to process the flow of paperwork efficiently, we need to clear the desk. *International Clear Your Desk! Day* takes place at the end of April every year, but this should not be the only day on which we make an effort to keep our paperwork under control. The clear-out should start today, with all the junk we have accumulated on the desk: glossy brochures, obsolete reports, magazines we will never read, memos we will never look at again. These items will have accumulated because they looked interesting at first glance and we put them aside telling ourselves we would look at them again when we had more time .

Once the desk has been cleared, it should remain clear. Many people say, 'I know I have lots of paper on the desk but it's only junk it's not real work!'. This junk however hides the important paperwork; it constantly distracts us and when we are procrastinating about an item of real work, this junk becomes infinitely more attractive and worthwhile. Operating a clear-desk policy does not mean that we will never be seen with paperwork on the desk again. It means that we should restrict our workspace to one project at a time. We should also try to avoid having a clear desk whilst having every other available space in the office piled high with paper.

The RAFT technique

The RAFT technique should be used to keep us afloat on the sea of paperwork. As soon as a piece of paper arrives we should make a definite decision about what to do with it and move on. There are in fact only four things we can do with a piece of paper that lands on the desk: **R**efer it, **A**ct on it, **F**ile it or **T**hrow it away.

Our referred paperwork should go straight in the out-tray, filing paperwork belongs in the filing system, junk should go straight in the bin and, where possible, our action paperwork should be dealt with straight away. Any actioned paperwork not dealt with immediately should go in a bring-forward file. We should have a place for everything and everything should go in its place.

Paperwork management checklist

- Be decisive when dealing with incoming paperwork
- Try to handle each piece of paper only once
- Avoid using a plethora of diaries and notepads
- Restrict the workspace to one project at a time
- Try to avoid high-rise trays on the desk
- Avoid using the in-tray as a storage space
- Use the RAFT technique
- Set up a bring-forward file for tracking unfinished paperwork
- Sort out the papers in our briefcase every day

Effective filing

The filing system, whether paper or electronic, is one of the most important management tools we have. We will concentrate on our paper files today, but the same general principles should be applied to computer files.

Unfortunately, filing is often seen as a clerical activity and not worthy of management attention. As a result, our filing systems tend to be poorly organised. Stacks of 'to file' paper build up on the desk, increasing the chances of items being mislaid. When we do file paperwork, it tends to be done in a haphazard fashion with the focus on getting the documents out of sight. We rarely give any thought to the question of finding them again.

To win back control of our filing system, we are first going to look at overcoming our tendency to hoard too much information. Then we will reorganise our files to make things easier to find.

De-junking the filing system

If we take a brief look through our files, we will probably find that most of their contents are obsolete: abandoned projects, glossy brochures, out-of-date reports, untouched reading material. In fact, studies have shown that approximately 85% of the information we keep will never be looked at again. Furthermore, a large proportion of the documents we file away are already stored somewhere else.

We should try to set aside 90 minutes today for purging our files. Working through the folders one by one we should consign to the bin all those items that:

a we will never get the time to look at;
b can easily be located elsewhere if needed;
c have a low pay-off attached to them.

If we are sufficiently ruthless, then the contents of our filing systems should be reduced by more than 50%. One rule that is adopted in many bureaucratic organisations is, 'Before throwing anything out, make a copy of it just in case you might need it again'. The rule should be taken with a pinch of salt, but it identifies the fear that many people have when throwing things away. We tell ourselves that someone is bound to need the document at some time in the future. If we talk to people who are ruthless about binning things, they will say that junked items are very rarely needed again and when that happens there is always a copy somewhere else.

Once the clear-out is complete, we should try to keep the quantity of files down by:

- Purging our files as we use them on a daily basis
- Asking others to retain copies of documents they send us
- Marking items with a discard date
- Never keeping copies of the same document in different files
- Asking others to keep paperwork concise
- Transferring infrequently-used files to archives

Reorganising the files

The better organised our files, the more likely we are to make use of the information we keep. There is an important filing maxim which states, 'If you don't know you have it, or you can't find it, then it's of absolutely no use to you'.

Very few of us have ever sat down and considered setting up a logical filing system. Our file headings are usually created with little thought and file folders are usually arranged at random in the drawer. We only have to watch ourselves and others trying to retrieve mislaid items from the filing cabinet to realise the importance of a good classification system.

There are six main ways of classifying information:

- By subject category
- Alphabetically
- By date
- By colour
- Geographically
- Numerically

We should experiment with different combinations of the above classifications until we develop a system that suits our way of working. Once we have decided on a suitable system, we will need physically to reorganise the files. The file management checklist below will help us in that endeavour.

File management checklist

- Use simple file headings
- Subdivide bulging folders
- Separate active files from infrequently-used records
- Put the filing cabinet within reach of the desk
- Don't allow stacks of filing to build up on the desk
- Use a classification system that can be trusted
- Purge files regularly

Group time management exercises

Individual paperwork wars are rarely successful. Our colleagues will become suspicious if we stop sending memos to them, and will be offended when we ask to be removed from their circulation lists. A company-wide *Clear Your Desk! Day* should be held and everyone encouraged to take part.

The best way to get the excess paperwork message across to our colleagues is to place a large box in the office in which everyone should place the unnecessary paper that arrives on the desk for a week. Then on the Monday of Office Productivity Week, a short meeting should be held during which the group should work through the stack of papers and determine how to eliminate this paperwork in future. Each person in our group or department should be asked to come up with three things they can do to reduce the low pay-off paperwork that:

a leaves the desk;
b arrives on the desk;
c is retained in their files.

Once we have our paperwork under control, we free up our time for more productive pursuits.

Tomorrow we shall concentrate on planning.

Planning

Today, we will look at planning on three levels. We will start off by looking into the future to set long-term business and personal goals. Next we will devise the action plans which provide the blueprint for turning our dreams into reality. Finally we will look at planning on a daily basis.

Planning

- Setting goals
- Devising action plans
- Daily plans

Planning is one of the most important time management skills. Our goals give us a sense of direction in both our personal and business lives. Those people who lack a clear vision of where they are going, spend a large proportion of their time reacting to the demands of others: urgent faxes, emergency telephone calls, asap memos and crisis meetings. No matter how efficient we are in dealing with those short-term demands it is difficult to be successful in the long term without plans. Accidental success is quite rare.

Setting goals

Successful companies have goals: to achieve the highest market share, for instance or to have the most efficient production line. Without these goals things would be chaotic. Successful athletes have goals: to break the world record, or to win a gold medal at the Olympics. Athletes would not get up to train at 5 a.m. on a cold winter's morning unless they had a clear vision of standing on the podium receiving a trophy. Successful managers also have clear goals.

Creative visualisation

Half an hour should be set aside today for an exercise in creative visualisation. We are going to sit back and dream of the future, banishing all negative thoughts from our minds. It is easy to be self-critical and to tell ourselves, 'I could never achieve that'. Long-term goals, such as running our own business, initially appear to be beyond our reach. In the next section we will look at breaking down our goals into manageable action plans. Once we have completed an action plan, all we have to do is concentrate on the next step. Before starting the creative visualisation process, we should ensure that we won't be disturbed.

Our look into the future should focus on both our work and our family lives. We should try to see ourselves in one, five, 10, 15 and 20 years from now. The questions overleaf will help us in that process.

Business goals

- What would I like to have achieved by the time I retire?
- What salary would I like to earn?
- Would I like to run my own business or become a senior manager in a large organisation?
- Should I remain in this country or work abroad?
- Would I benefit from further education?
- What business skills do I need to develop?
- What industry would I really like to work in?
- What is my ideal job?
- What professional organisations should I join?

Personal goals

- What hobbies/special interests would I like to pursue?
- Where would I like to live?
- Do I need to spend more time with the family?
- What parts of the world would I like to see?
- Should I learn a new language?
- Do I need to adopt a healthier diet?
- Could I improve my level of fitness?
- What sort of home would I like to live in?

As we visualise our future achievements we should write them down as goals in our time management notebook.

We should hold a creative visualisation session every six months because certain goals may have been reached or, due to circumstances beyond our control, certain goals may have changed slightly. Each time we achieve a goal, we should set another one so that we are always working towards a more fulfilling business and personal life.

Devising action plans

Unless we make definite plans we cannot hope to turn our dreams into reality. The action plans we devise for each of our goals will provide step-by-step guidelines for achieving those goals.

The benefits of action plans are clear to all those who use them.

Action plans:

- Break down daunting goals into achievable steps
- Motivate us to achieve our goals
- Make implementation of ideas easier
- Provide us with a useful overview
- Enable us to focus on the important rather than the urgent
- Provide a benchmark against which we can judge progress
- Help us to anticipate problems

The steps we need to take to achieve each of our goals should be written down on the relevant page in our time management notebook. If we have a goal to be MD of a large company we should work back from the goal and ask ourselves, 'What do I need to do to get there?'. Any major steps we need to take should be broken down into smaller more achievable steps. We should also set a deadline for achieving our goal and deadlines for achieving each step along the way.

An important question we need to ask ourselves is, 'What will it cost to achieve the goal?'. There may be a substantial financial cost involved, such as investing in an MBA programme. There may also be a personal cost involved. If we are going to set up our own business, it may mean we have less time to spend with family and friends. So, we need to weigh up the cost of achieving our goals against their pay-off.

Daily plans

Once our action plans are complete, we need to come back
to the present and look at compiling daily plans or 'to-do'
lists.

Daily plans:

- Enable us to plan our work sensibly
- Act as reminders
- Unclutter the mind
- Help us to keep track of deadlines
- Motivate us to get things done
- Help us to focus on priorities

Eight steps to effective daily plans
We are now going to look at a straightforward process for
compiling daily plans. The medium on which we capture
our plans is not as important as the process. Electronic to-do
lists, index card systems, personal organisers, or desk diaries
can all be used effectively.

1 Five minute planning period
At the end of each day we should spend five minutes
planning the next day. As we turn the page of our diary
there should already be a number of things to do,
commitments and action plan steps which have been carried
forward from previous days. For example:

To do	Priority	Completed	Delegate	Time
Call John				
Finish marketing report				
Read article				
Arrange meeting with M.G.				

2 Carry forward today's unfinished activities
We should tick off the activities that have been completed
today and transfer unfinished activities to tomorrow's list or
to a future day's list if appropriate. If we frequently find
ourselves with a large number of unfinished tasks at the end
of the day, we are probably trying to squeeze too much into
the day. We should therefore leave greater room for
unexpected events.

To do	Priority	Completed	Delegate	Time
Call John				
Finish marketing report				
Read article				
Arrange meeting with M.G.				

To do	Priority	Completed	Delegate	Time

Call T.D.
Reply to B.C.G letter
Finalise budgets
Send file to A.C.

3 Plan tomorrow's activities
Taking account of our scheduled activities such as meetings and appointments, list the activities to tackle tomorrow.

To do	Priority	Completed	Delegate	Time

Call John
Finish marketing
 report
Read article
Arrange meeting
 with M.G.
Call T.D.
Reply to B.C.G letter
Finalise budgets
Send file to A.C.
Copy for brochure
Check travel
 arrangements
Send slides to
 bureau
Prepare mailshot
Read next chapter
 of this book

4 Include goal-related activities

We should always include activities that will lead to us achieving our long-term goals. When busy we tend to react to the urgent items rather than the items that will benefit us in the long run. It is important therefore to always include goal related activities on our to-do list.

To do	Priority	Completed	Delegate	Time
Call John				
Finish marketing report				
Read article				
Arrange meeting with M.G.				
Call T.D.				
Reply to B.C.G letter				
Finalise budgets				
Send file to A.C.				
Copy for brochure				
Check travel arrangements				
Send slides to bureau				
Prepare mailshot				
Read next chapter of this book				
Co. MBA sponsorship?				
Buy French tapes				

5 Prioritise things to do

Working through the list, we should prioritise each activity. Our goal-related activities should always be assigned an 'A' priority; items with associated deadlines are the same, as are items with high pay-offs. 'B' priorities will include those items we would like to get done but which can be delayed if we don't have the time.

To do	Priority	Completed	Delegate	Time
Call John	B			
Finish marketing report	B			
Read article	B			
Arrange meeting with M.G.	A			
Call T.D.	B			
Reply to B.C.G letter	B			
Finalise budgets	A			
Send file to A.C.	B			
Copy for brochure	A			
Check travel arrangements	B			
Send slides to bureau	A			
Prepare mailshot	B			
Read next chapter of this book	A			
Co. MBA sponsorship ?	A			
Buy French tapes	A			

6 Delegate activities

No manager should ever get bogged down in a mountain of paperwork because it can always be delegated. Working through our to-do list we should ask ourselves who the best person is to deal with each item. In delegating, we should be seeking to develop the skills of the people around us rather than dumping work on them.

To do	Priority	Completed	Delegate	Time
Call John	B			
Finish marketing report	B		J.D.	
Read article	B			
Arrange meeting with M.G.	A			
Call T.D.	B			
Reply to B.C.G letter	B			
Finalise budgets	A		J.D.	
Send file to A.C.	B			
Copy for brochure	A			
Check travel arrangements	B		A.H.	
Send slides to bureau	A			
Prepare mailshot	B			
Read next chapter of this book	A			
Co. MBA sponsorship?	A			
Buy French tapes	A			

7 Estimate the length of time each task requires

This process is difficult until we get used to it. When we have totalled up our estimates along with our scheduled activities they should not add up to more than 75% of the working day. It is important not to try to plan every minute; we need to be flexible in order to accommodate the unexpected.

To do	Priority	Completed	Delegate	Time
Call John	B			10
Finish marketing report	B		J.D.	60
Read article	B			15
Arrange meeting with M.G.	A			5
Call T.D.	B			10
Reply to B.C.G letter	B			20
Finalise budgets	A		J.D.	5
Send file to A.C.	B			5
Copy for brochure	A			30
Check travel arrangements	B		A.H.	5
Send slides to bureau	A			10
Prepare mailshot	B			20
Read next chapter of this book	A			60
Co. MBA sponsorship?	A			10
Buy French tapes	A			5

8 Work through mail and make additions to list
Tomorrow morning our mail will invariably throw up a
number of important things to do. These should be added to
our list.

To do	Priority	Completed	Delegate	Time
Call John	B			10
Finish marketing report	B		J.D.	60
Read article	B			15
Arrange meeting with M.G.	A			5
Call T.D.	B			10
Reply to B.C.G letter	B			20
Finalise budgets	A		J.D.	5
Send file to A.C.	B			5
Copy for brochure	A			30
Check travel arrangements	B		A.H.	5
Send slides to bureau	A			10
Prepare mailshot	B			20
Read next chapter of this book	A			60
Co. MBA sponsorship?	A			10
Buy French tapes	A			5
Check invoice	*B*			*10*
Discuss complaint with sales	*A*			*20*
				295

Once our to-do list is complete we are ready to attack the day. The temptation is often to start on the quick and easy activities, ticking off many items on the list. The only effective way to work however, is to tackle our activities in order of priority. As a general rule, we should not tackle a B priority item unless all our A priorities have been completed. It can be useful to set aside a 'quiet hour' in the day when we know we will not be disturbed for tackling important items. Where possible, similar activities should be grouped together: telephone calls, correspondence, or delegation to secretary.

Group time management exercises

On the Tuesday of Office Productivity Week, a one-hour meeting should be held to discuss effective planning. Each member of the group should be asked in advance to identify one of their business goals and to prepare an action plan for achieving it. These action plans can be discussed and fine-tuned during the meeting.

Each member of the group should also be asked to use the eight-step daily planning process for at least one day before the Tuesday of Office Productivity Week. A group meeting can then be held during which individuals can discuss any problems that have arisen in using to-do lists and the benefits they have brought. Different members of the group may have conflicting priorities and the group meeting is the perfect opportunity to resolve them.

The pay-off from our plans is never immediate and that is why many people adopt a reactive approach to time management. If we focus on our urgent and immediate tasks we will always receive an instant pay-off. A longer term pro-active approach will delay the pay-off but it will always be much greater. A useful principle to bear in mind when working through our to-do list is the 80:20 rule: 80% of our results come from 20% of our activities.

Tomorrow, we will look at managing meetings.

Managing meetings

Most managers spend somewhere between 30 and 50% of their working lives in meetings: drop-in visitors, committee meetings, recruitment interviews, brainstorming sessions, crisis meetings and conferences.

Today, we are going to explore ways of maximising that time investment. First of all we will try to identify some of the factors behind unproductive meetings. Then, starting afresh, we will look at what should be done before, during and after our meetings, whether as chairperson or attendee, to make them more productive. We will examine checklists that can be followed for all meetings, whether they are one-to-one discussions or more formal gatherings.

Managing meetings

- Why do meetings go wrong?
- What to do before meetings
- What to do during meetings
- What to do after meetings

As a means of communicating, meetings can prove very useful. They enable us to:

- Transfer information and receive feedback
- Generate new ideas
- Build consensus for a decision or course of action
- Combine expertise to solve problems

Things can go wrong, however, as hinted at in the business adage, 'In all your parks and all your cities you'll find no statues of committees'.

Why do meetings go wrong?

We should set aside about 20 minutes to evaluate our current meeting management skills. The first question we need to ask ourselves is, 'What proportion of my time is spent in meetings?'. Next, we should ask ourselves, 'What proportion of that time is wasted?'. Thinking back over the meetings we have attended in the past few weeks we should explore the following areas:

- How much did the meetings cost?
- Were the costs of attending the meetings greater than the benefits gained?
- Were the meetings adequately planned?
- How many meetings were delayed because of late-comers ?
- Did the meetings frequently last longer than expected?
- Were there problems with equipment and facilities?
- Did I make worthwhile contributions to the meetings?
- Did other participants make worthwhile contributions?
- Did the meetings tend to wander away from the agenda?
- Were decisions, taken during the meeting, followed up?

Now that we have identified the potential pitfalls, we will turn our attention to making our meetings more productive. We will start with the meeting preparations.

What to do before the meeting as chairperson

Whether guiding a formal meeting or arranging an informal chat, it is our responsibility to make sure that the right people are in the right place at the right time and have received the relevant background information. The checklist below should be followed before each meeting that we organise.

Chairperson's checklist

- Is the meeting really necessary?
- What are the alternatives to meeting face to face?
- What are the objectives of the meeting?
- Who is needed to ensure that these objectives are achieved?
- What will be the pay-off from achieving the objectives?
- What will the meeting cost?
- What equipment/facilities are needed for the meeting?
- If an agenda is required has it been prepared/distributed?
- Are all the attendees clear about the start time and location of the meeting?
- Have attendees received all the relevant background information?
- Do all the participants need to be present for the whole meeting?

At first, we may find working through the checklist a bit laborious, especially for smaller meetings, but over time, the questions will become ingrained in our memory. Running through the questions mentally will become a matter of habit.

What are the alternatives to a meeting?
How many of the meetings we attended in the past week could have been replaced by a brief chat, a memo, a quick telephone call, a decision by the person in charge? Could the issues have been added to the agenda of another meeting? Before arranging any meeting we should look at all the other alternatives.

The meeting's purpose
We should clearly define the the meeting's objectives, and communicate them to participants when arranging the meeting. This gives others the chance to prepare in advance and ensures that people do not have to sit through an irrelevant meeting because they thought it was going to be about something else.

The meeting pay-off
Once we have set the objectives for the meeting, we need to ask what the pay-off from achieving each objective will be. The pay-offs will enable us to prioritise the agenda and focus on the important items. The total meeting pay-off should be weighed against the meeting cost to see if it is a worthwhile exercise.

NICE AGENDA !

Preparing the agenda

As the number of participants in a meeting increases, so the need for an agenda grows. The agenda should be kept brief and uncluttered. The agenda items should be positive and achievement oriented, i.e. 'To find a solution to the distribution problem', rather than 'To discuss distribution problems'. The highest pay-off items should be placed at the top of the agenda so that if we run out of time, the major issues will have been covered.

What to do before the meeting as attendee

As meeting participants, we need to evaluate the necessity of attending the meeting and to be well prepared. Instead of attending, we can save time by talking to people who have attended or by looking at the minutes afterwards.

Attendee's checklist

- Do I really need to attend the meeting?
- Is there an alternative to the meeting?
- Am I sure of the correct time/location of the meeting?
- Have I arranged my schedule so that I will get to the meeting on time?
- What do I want to contribute to the meeting?
- What do I want to get out of the meeting?
- What background paperwork do I need to tackle?
- Do I need to attend all of the meeting or just part of it?

What to do during the meeting as chairperson

As chairperson, we need to be aware of the destructive forces that can make meetings unproductive. We will look at some of the more common forces, along with strategies for coping with them.

Late-comers

We should never reward the late-comers and punish the punctual participants by holding meetings back until everyone is present. If we are lax about start times, we give participants licence to make extra phone calls or to chat with colleagues in the corridor before the meeting. We should, without exception, start our meetings on time. As soon as the meeting starts, the door should be closed. As late-comers

arrive, we should never interrupt the meeting to bring them up to date on what has been discussed.

Hidden agendas
At the start of the meeting, attendees should be asked what they personally want to get out of the meeting. We will then get the hidden issues and concerns out into the open where they can be addressed.

Rambling discussions
The only way to stop long-winded or irrelevant contributions is to interrupt. We should wait for someone to take a breath, jump in, briefly summarise the point being made, and move on.

Low participation
We should actively try to encourage the participation of attendees by reacting positively to contributions. There is no quicker way to silence a group than to be over critical. If someone with potentially useful contributions is silent, we

should ask them directly for their ideas. Asking people to confer in pairs or smaller groups is another useful technique for getting things started.

Interruptions

There is a famous story about a US senator in a meeting with the President. The phone was ringing continuously and the President was getting involved in a protracted conversation each time he picked it up. Eventually, the senator left the room and called the oval office extension. He immediately got the President's attention.

We should arrange for all calls to be put on hold for the duration of our meetings. 'Do not disturb' signs should also be used for office doors indicating the time that the meeting will be over. If someone does break through our initial barriers, we should arrange a time when we can get back to them.

Arguments

If people are arguing unproductively during meetings, we should suggest that their discussions be continued outside the meeting. If that is not possible, we should acknowledge the differing points of view and ask participants to focus on a solution. In larger meetings, we can bring arguments to an end by asking for a show of hands on the issue.

Group indecisiveness

There is no point having meetings where lots of things are discussed but nothing is decided. After each item on the agenda has been discussed, we need to summarise the decision taken, any follow-up actions and deadlines. If

possible, we should produce an instant action summary during the meeting and distribute photocopies to participants as they leave.

Decision/action to be taken	Person responsible	Deadline
Letter to be sent	J.D.	12/5
Report on product launch	G.H.	22/5
Sales conference details	J.D.	22/5
New computer system	M.G.	28/5

On paper, many of the suggestions for controlling meetings look straightforward. In the middle of a meeting however, they will appear a lot more difficult, and the easiest option is to do nothing. We need to practise these techniques, meeting after meeting, until we get them right. If we learn how to control destructive forces, our meetings will be dynamic, productive and enjoyable.

Chairperson's checklist

- Always start on time
- Set out the objectives for the meeting
- Stay positive throughout the meeting
- Follow up actions from the last meeting
- Decide who will take the minutes
- Encourage participation from reserved attendees
- Silence sidetrackers
- Keep the discussion focused on the agenda
- Adhere strictly to the agenda timetable
- Summarise decisions/actions to be taken as the meeting progresses, and again at the end
- Ensure that all the items on the agenda are covered
- Finish the meeting on time.

What to do during meetings as attendee

As participants at meetings, we should always try to be constructive. If we act counterproductively, we are wasting our own time as well as that of the other participants.

Attendee's checklist

- Contribute constructively to the meeting
- Restrict contributions to agenda items
- Focus on the meeting's objectives
- Be clear about any follow-up steps to take
- Avoid private discussions during the meeting

What to do after meetings as chairperson

What happens after the meeting, ultimately determines whether or not the meeting has been a success.

As soon as the meeting is over the chairperson should quickly work through the questions below. In certain circumstances it can be useful to evaluate the meeting with the participants.

Chairperson's checklist

- Has the meeting been a success?
- Were the right participants present?
- Were all the items on the agenda covered?
- How should unfinished items be dealt with?
- Do I need to distribute meeting minutes?
- What should I do differently next time?
- Could we have achieved the same results without a meeting?

What to do after meetings as attendee

After the meeting has finished, we should transfer any follow-up actions into our to-do list and ask ourselves the questions below.

Attendee's checklist

- Was my participation in the meeting really necessary?
- Am I clear about any follow-up actions I need to take?
- Did I contribute constructively to the meeting?
- What should I do differently next time?

Group time management exercises

On the Wednesday of our Office Productivity Week we should hold a one-hour meeting on the subject of managing meetings. Participants should be asked to prepare in advance and contribute constructively to the meeting. Some members of the group should be asked to observe the meeting and judge each person on their contribution. Once the meeting is over, participants should be asked to evaluate its success according to the checklists in this chapter. Could individuals have been better prepared? What destructive forces were present during the meeting? Is everyone clear about the follow-up actions?

Meetings can be a productive way of getting things done but they can also be an unnecessary drain on our time. If we pay attention to getting things right, the rewards throughout our careers will be enormous.

Tomorrow, we shall take a look at project management.

Managing projects

Today, we are going to look at fine-tuning our project management skills. There are three stages in managing a project: planning, controlling and evaluating. If we fail to manage these three stages effectively, the project may well end up in the project graveyard. A quick glance through the papers on the desk or gathering dust in the filing system will invariably reveal many projects which we started enthusiastically but which were never completed.

Project management

- Planning
- Control
- Evaluation and review

A project is a series of interrelated tasks leading to a definite end. We spend a large proportion of our time juggling projects ranging from writing a report to launching a new product. Smaller projects can be dealt with by writing the individual tasks on our daily to-do lists, while larger projects require a more sophisticated approach. It is these larger projects on which we will concentrate today.

Working through this chapter provides us with the ideal opportunity to plan a project which we are about to take on. After reading the chapter once, we should choose a project and work through it according to the principles outlined. We should also compile a list of all upcoming projects in our time management notebook, and schedule time for planning them properly.

Before going on to look at the three stages of project management, it will benefit us to look at the 10 most common reasons why projects fail.

1 Taking on too much
2 Inadequate planning
3 Project costs outweighing benefits
4 Ineffective delegation of project tasks
5 Procrastination
6 Failure to spot potential problems
7 Focus on more immediate, but lower pay-off, items
8 Lack of overview
9 Lack of a clearly defined objective
10 Poor communication between members of project team

Looking back over the last three unsuccessful projects we took on, we should compile a list of the reasons why they failed. Once that has been completed, we can look at ways of ensuring the success of our future projects.

Planning

The more time we spend planning the project, the easier its implementation will be. With project management, we need to be pro-active rather than re-active. We need to anticipate problems rather than waste time trying to sort them out once they have occurred.

There are five major stages in planning a project. Each stage should be followed as we plan a current project.

1 Identify the objective
The objective provides the focus for all the individual tasks that must be performed as part of the project. It should be stated clearly and concisely because, if the objective is stated ambiguously, then the different members of the project team may end up working towards different ends. The questions below will help us to identify the objective. A project overview page should be set up in our time management notebook for each project we undertake and the answers to these questions written down.

- When the project has been completed I will have achieved . . .?
- What problems will the project help to solve?
- How will the project be completed?
- Who else will be involved in completing the project?
- What is the scope of the project?
- How long will it take to complete the project?

2   Cost-benefit analysis

Many projects are undertaken without proper consideration of the costs involved and then when these costs escalate alarmingly during the project, it has to be abandoned. For the project we are currently planning, we need to examine the costs of undertaking it, as well as the rewards to be gained from completing it. These rewards may be financial in terms of increased revenue or decreased costs. The intangible rewards which cannot be measured in financial terms should also be considered.

- What tangible benefits will result from the project?
- What intangible benefits will result from the project?
- What are the costs involved in completing the project?
- Do the benefits outweigh the costs?

In our time management notebook, we should compile a list of costs on one side of the page and a list of benefits on the other. The project should only proceed when we are satisfied that the benefits outweigh the costs.

3 Break the project down into individual tasks
Sometimes, when we are faced with a large project it can seem overwhelming. Where do we make a start? Often, we make a start, but not at the beginning, and then leave key tasks until it is too late and we have a crisis on our hands. On one page in our time management notebook, we should break down the project into its individual tasks. Start with the major tasks and break them down into smaller tasks until everything that needs to be done has been identified.

For each individual task, we need to ask, 'What could possibly go wrong?'. The answer to this question will help us to set up contingency plans.

4 Schedule the tasks
Alongside each individual task we should write down an estimate of how long it will take to complete. Next we should decide on an appropriate deadline for each task. Many tasks can be completed at the same time, while others may have to be performed sequentially. We should be realistic here and allow for delays. It might take us 10 minutes to obtain an item of information from a colleague, but it may take us a week to arrange a meeting with them. Once we have completed our scheduling, we can set a deadline for the project. Finally, the deadlines should be transferred to our to-do lists for the relevant day. Key project tasks which, if not completed will cause the project to fail, should be highlighted on our to-do lists.

5 Delegate tasks where appropriate
Many of the projects we undertake will involve us working with others. This means that the project workload will be

spread out, and we will also benefit from the input of others at the planning stage. When delegating tasks, we should negotiate a deadline for their completion and write it down on the relevant to-do list.

Control

Project control is the process of monitoring projects to ensure they are on track, and taking corrective action where necessary.

The project overview in our time management notebooks will prove invaluable during this stage. When we are dealing with a large number of projects, essential tasks may slip through the cracks. We should constantly refer back to our list of tasks on our project overview page and tick them off as they are completed. If there is a lot of time-sensitive paperwork involved in the project, we will need to use a bring-forward system for keeping track of everything.

One or more project files should be set up and kept in an accessible place. We should purge the file after each major stage of the project has been completed, so that we are not constantly shuffling through piles of unnecessary paper whilst looking for something important. Many people leave all their project paperwork on the desk and say, 'I have people coming into the office all the time to discuss things, so I need to have everything where I can lay my hands on it'. However, this method means that important documents often get buried, and the papers relating to different projects get scattered around and mixed up.

The most important part of project control is to avoid being distracted by the urgent but unimportant items that land on the desk every day. A prioritised to-do list is essential here. We should constantly monitor ourselves to ensure that we are focused on the high pay-off project tasks.

Control checklist

- Monitor scheduled project tasks on a daily basis
- Always assign an 'A' priority to project tasks
- Keep track of delegation deadlines using the diary
- Periodically refer back to the project overview page
- Use a bring-forward file for time-sensitive paperwork
- Keep project paperwork together in a project file

Evaluation and review

Reviewing completed projects is a brief but essential exercise. During the planning stage, the evaluation should be scheduled as the final project task. If the project has not gone according to plan, the review enables us to analyse what went wrong so that we can avoid similar problems in the future. If the project has been successful, the review enables us to identify why things went well, to acknowledge the positive contribution of others, and to congratulate ourselves. Any lessons we learn during the completion of a project should be noted down on a special page in our time-management notebook. This page can then be reviewed during the planning stage of future projects.

When evaluating the project, we should ask ourselves the following questions:

Project review checklist

- Was the project objective achieved?
- Was the project completed by the deadline?
- If not, why not?
- Was adequate time assigned to planning?
- Were all the project tasks identified beforehand?
- What avoidable crises occurred during the project?
- What problems could have been avoided by prior action?
- Were the right people involved in the project?
- Was everyone motivated to complete the project?
- Was the project completed within the allocated budget?
- What would we do differently if we could start again?

Finally, we should rate the overall success of the project on a scale of 1-10.

Group time management exercises

On the Thursday of our Office Productivity Week we should turn our attention to projects. During the one-hour session, the group should evaluate a number of projects that have been undertaken in the previous month: what factors contributed to the success or failure of these projects? Each member of the group should be asked to identify a project they are about to undertake and should explain to the others their planning process:

1   Defining the objective;
2   Cost-benefit analysis;
3   Breaking the project down into individual tasks;
4   Scheduling the tasks;
5   Delegating the tasks.

We are now equipped with the right tools for tackling any future projects.

Tomorrow, we shall learn how to tame the telephone.

Taming the telephone

Today we are going to look at ways of taming the telephone. First of all we will look at telephone mismanagement and the traits of the telephone junkie. We will then look at techniques for controlling our incoming calls and for making our outgoing calls more productive.

Taming the telephone

- The telephone trap
- The telephone junkie
- Incoming calls
- Outgoing calls

The telephone trap

The telephone is an invaluable management tool. It allows us to communicate instantly with people anywhere in the world. It is more cost-effective than travelling to a meeting and quicker than written communications. There is a downside, however, in that we are instantly accessible to anyone who wishes to speak to us regardless of how unimportant the issue or inconvenient the time. We can say 'no' to a meeting and throw a low pay-off letter in the bin but as soon as we pick up the telephone and hear, 'Let me tell you about our new photocopier', 'About the letter I sent you', or 'I just rang to see how things are going', we are trapped. Someone else is determining how we spend our time.

The secret of good telephone management lies in eliminating, or cutting short, the junk calls while getting the most from the important ones.

The telephone junkie

Telephone junkies have a detrimental effect on everyone in the office: too many unnecessary calls are made, too much time is spent on each call, important calls are not returned, items agreed upon during calls are not followed up... the list is endless. We all exhibit the traits of the telephone junkie from time to time. The questionnaire opposite will help us to determine how often.

Telephone junkie questionnaire

Do I:

	Sometimes	Always	Never
rush to answer the phone as soon as it rings?	☐	☐	☐
spend longer on calls than is really necessary?	☐	☐	☐
have to make calls twice because there was something I forgot to say?	☐	☐	☐
allow telephone calls to interrupt my meetings?	☐	☐	☐
dial numbers and then forget who I called?	☐	☐	☐
drop what I'm doing when I remember a call I need to make?	☐	☐	☐
not screen my calls even when there is someone available to do so?	☐	☐	☐
spend more than 30 seconds dealing with unsolicited sales callers?	☐	☐	☐
finish calls without covering the topics I want to discuss?	☐	☐	☐
scatter my outgoing calls randomly throughout the day?	☐	☐	☐
write down messages on the handiest piece of paper at the time?	☐	☐	☐
forget to pass telephone messages on to others?	☐	☐	☐

Scoring the questionnaire:

For each 'sometimes' answer, we should score ourselves 1 point; for each 'always' answer, 3 points, and 0 points for each 'never' answer. A score of 16 or more puts us into the telephone junkie category and we need to sit back and evaluate how we are using the telephone. Why are we not

using it productively? What needs to change before we can gain control over the telephone? Even a score of less than 16 means that the telephone probably rules our lives from time to time. The questionnaire will have helped in identifying those areas we specifically need to work on today and in the future. We should use our score as a benchmark to gauge our improvement over the coming weeks and months.

Incoming calls

The telephone rings continuously during the day. A certain proportion of our incoming calls bring good news or provide useful information, while the remainder are unnecessary. Unfortunately we cannot tell before picking up the phone which calls are important. Managing incoming calls is therefore partly a damage limitation exercise. We need to keep the unwanted calls brief, and the important calls productive .

Most of us underestimate the length of time we spend on the phone during the day. Setting up a telephone log, as shown below, will therefore be a revealing exercise. Every call we receive today should be noted along with its duration and pay-off. Our time management notebook should be used for this exercise.

Telephone log: incoming calls

Date:

Time	From	Re:	Duration	Pay-off
9.20	sales	photocopier	5 mins	low
9.50	S. West	set up sales meeting	17 mins	med
10.30	D. Martin	in meeting, asked to call back	2 mins	low
11.00	M. George	query on memo	11 mins	low
11.20	client	sales order	13 mins	high
11.48	sales	training course	4 mins	low
:	:	:	:	:
:	:	:	:	:
4.50	A. Smith	tennis game	15 mins	low

Total time spent on incoming calls: 2 hrs 5 mins

At the end of the day we need to set aside five minutes to analyse our calls and ask ourselves the following questions:

- How many unexpected calls did I receive?
- How many unwanted calls did I receive?
- How many calls lasted longer than necessary?
- How many calls could have been dealt with by someone else?
- How many calls interrupted me when I was busy with a high pay-off item?
- How many calls could have been screened out?

It pays to practise techniques for keeping our junk calls brief. In our time management notebook, we should note down at least three excuses we can use, such as, 'I'm in the middle of a meeting right now can you tell me very quickly what you want', 'I have a taxi waiting for me', or 'I have a conference call booked in about two minutes'.

When the telephone interrupts our work, many of us have a tendency to scribble notes on the nearest piece of paper, whether it is a letter or an open report. This habit creates problems for us when we need to go back and find someone's telephone number or check on the price we quoted. Which bit of paper were we using at the time? Where did it go? For important colleagues or contacts, we should set up an index card or a page in our personal organiser. Each time they ring, we can turn to their page and immediately see what the last conversation was about or if there are any items we need to discuss with them. The key points of the current conversation can be captured and retrieved quickly if we need to refer to them.

The checklist below outlines 10 important techniques for managing incoming calls. We should try to use them all throughout the day. If we have problems with any of the techniques we should develop strategies for overcoming them.

Techniques for managing incoming calls

- Put phone on divert or DND when busy
- Set aside a quiet hour during which we will not take calls
- Ask for all calls to be put on hold during meetings
- Be polite, firm and brief with unwanted sales callers
- Ask people to call at particular times when we are less busy
- Avoid tackling peripheral tasks while on the phone
- Avoid taking notes on loose bits of paper
- Arrange for calls to be screened whenever possible
- Ask the receptionist not to give out names to cold callers
- Make a list of excuses for keeping calls short

Outgoing calls

Outgoing calls are more manageable. We can decide who we wish to speak to, when we make the call, what we want to say, and we also have greater control over its duration. A telephone log should be set up for outgoing calls in our time management notebook.

Telephone log: outgoing calls

Date:

Time	To	Re:	Duration	Pay-off
10.20	Personnel	job advert	8 mins	med
12.00	Personnel	forgot to ask about salary details	3 mins	low
:	:		:	:
:	:	:	:	:
3.20	J. Coates	arrange meeting	24 mins	med

Total time spent on outgoing calls: 1 hr 38 mins

Towards the end of the day, when our outgoing calls telephone log has been completed, we should ask ourselves the following questions for each call:

- Was the telephone the best way of getting the message across?
- Did I achieve my objective?
- Did I waste too much time on small-talk?
- Did the call drift into low pay-off areas?
- Did the call last longer than anticipated?
- Was there anything I forgot to say?

Planning the call

Most outgoing calls are made on the spur of the moment. We are sitting at the desk and we suddenly remember we have to call someone. We pick up the phone without thinking and launch into the call. As a result we forget things we want to say, we put things across badly, and we fail to get the information we need.

Before making any call we should ask ourselves: what information do I need to pass on? What information do I need to obtain? What is the best way to get the message across? What papers do I need to have to hand for the call?

Making the call

We should treat each call as a mini-meeting. We should ensure that we get our own message across, and that we capture the other person's ideas. It is a good idea to summarise quickly the points made during the call, to make sure there is no confusion. We should block off time in our diary once or twice a day and make our outgoing calls together. Grouping our calls will motivate us to be brief and to the point. Our calls should also be prioritised and then made in order of priority. We should also create a sense of urgency with our lower pay-off calls by setting a definite time limit.

After the call

Any action points that arise as a result of our discussions should be followed up immediately or written down on a to-do list.

The checklist below provides guidelines which should be followed for each outgoing call made. We should block off

time in our diary for tomorrow and make a list of all the calls we need to make.

Checklist for managing outgoing calls

- Plan calls as if attending a meeting
- Make outgoing calls in blocks
- Prioritise calls
- Set limits on the duration of each call
- Collect relevant documents before the call
- Summarise discussions before the end of the call

Group time management exercises

Each member of the group should be asked to complete the telephone junkie questionnaire along with the incoming and outgoing telephone logs. During the group discussion, the members of the group should identify techniques for managing calls more effectively.

Most people reading this chapter at work will have been constantly interrupted by unnecessary telephone calls. The techniques in this chapter should help to reduce this problem and make the telephone a more productive management tool.

To end the week, we shall review the time management techniques covered, and look at a few additional timesaving tips.

Additional time tips and review

Today we are going to review the topics explored so far this week and look at some additional time management techniques that will improve our time management skills further.

Additional time tips

Time and travel
Executives are spending more and more of their time travelling, both nationally and internationally. The time spent travelling can eat into our productive working time. Careful preparation before major trips is essential. Some time should be spent writing down a list of objectives for the trip and then collecting together all the necessary paperwork. We should keep a travel file for collecting together all our travel documents, and prepare a special file containing the background information for meetings we will be attending. During the trip, it is essential to keep all our papers under control, because the chaos is very difficult to unravel when we get back to the office. At the end of each day, we should review our paperwork for the day, try to deal with any action points on the spot, and discard any unnecessary documents.

On long or short trips, we can always make use of our travel time. It is an ideal opportunity to catch up on our reading. Magazines, newsletters, reports, routine correspondence should be collected in a reading file so that we can catch up when travelling. If we find it difficult to read while travelling, we can substitute the spoken word; most of the

business bestsellers are now available in audio format. As
portable computers become more widely available, we can
use our travel time even more productively, catching up on
correspondence or writing reports.

Speed reading

A useful technique for coping with the mountain of
paperwork is speed reading. Whenever possible we should
ask for concise paperwork, but where we have no control
over the thickness of a report, we need to be able to extract
the important information in the minimum amount of time.
We should always try to read sensibly: look for summaries
and conclusions, skim through documents to get the key
headings, and look for diagrams and illustrations to get the
overall picture. If we need to read the complete document,
the guidelines below will prove useful. We should take a
report currently lying on the desk and try to put these
guidelines into practice.

- Use a guide such as a finger or card as we move down the page
- Focus on the middle of each line rather than moving the eyes along it
- Read groups of words together rather than one after the other
- Avoid saying the words to ourselves as they are read

Perfectionism can be dangerous

In some cases, it is wise to pay attention to detail but in many cases it can be counterproductive. To get something 90% right will often suffice. If we spend time getting internal memos, reports, presentations or projects 100% right it often means that something more important is left in the in-tray. Furthermore, the extra time we spend on any one task is rarely worth the extra pay-off. The law of diminishing returns comes into play. If we are preparing something for someone else, we should agree on a level of performance that is acceptable. There is absolutely no benefit to the company if we spend an extra 30 minutes printing an internal report again to correct a few spelling mistakes. If others are drafting letters or reports for us, we should try to avoid editing their work. We have to appreciate that others may say things in a slightly different way to us, but which is no less valid.

The KISS principle

The KISS (Keep It Short and Simple) principle should be applied to everything we do. It is a waste of time holding a meeting if the matter can be resolved by a quick phone call.

There is little value in writing a 10-page report where two pages are all that is necessary. There is no need to send a memo to someone when we bump into them several times a day. Introducing a form is unnecessary if the information asked for can be obtained elsewhere. We should go back and look at the time logs we completed on Sunday and ask ourselves which activities would not have been undertaken if the KISS principle was used.

Decisiveness

If there are piles of paper lying on and around the desk, it is a sure sign that we are indecisive. Each document that is currently lying in our in-tray represents a decision we have not yet made. Habitually postponing decisions means that we will handle the same bits of paper again and again without acting on them: a luxury that few of us can afford. Deadlines and opportunities will pass us by as we ponder over difficult decisions.

We should experiment with instant decisions and see what happens. We will probably find these decisions are just as effective. We sometimes tell ourselves that we need to wait for more information as an excuse for delaying decisions. Often this information cannot be obtained, and even if it does arrive on the desk, it doesn't change the decision we would have made. We often put off decisions because they may have unpleasant consequences, but an uncomfortable decision is better than no decision at all.

Adapt to suit the environment

No matter how effectively we plan, we must always be prepared to adapt to changing circumstances. Often we can predict likely changes in advance. If we get a lot of phone calls in the morning, we should not schedule an urgent task for that time. If our boss delegates work late in the day, we should try to get our 'A' priority work done before then so that we are not swamped with work. If we face a lot of genuine crises, then we should only plan a small proportion of the day.

Delegation

Delegation is the art of getting things done through others. As we progress through our careers, we will find it necessary to rely more and more on our colleagues to get things done for us. Many managers fear delegation and the loss of control it brings, but it is essential to free up our own time for higher pay-off activities.

Five steps to effective delegation

1 Communicate clearly what needs to be done
2 Agree a deadline for completion of the task
3 Let go of the task and trust the delegatee
4 Reward successful completion of the task
5 Be considerate and avoid dumping tasks on others

In our time management notebook we should spend five minutes writing down all the activities that should be delegated to others.

Adopt a positive outlook on life
A positive outlook on life can only increase our chances of being successful. Excuses can always be found for the problems that confront us. With a negative outlook we spend our time complaining and blaming others for our problems instead of working to find a solution. Of course, it is not always easy to be positive, but in the long term we

will be rewarded. A positive outlook will also motivate the people around us to get things done. Looking back over the past week, we should mentally list all the time management problems that we blamed on others, rather than asking what we could do to eliminate them.

Review

We are now going to look back over the week and review our performance day by day. We should already have noticed many improvements in our management of time, and highlighted areas which need more effort. For each day we need to ask ourselves, 'What successes did I have?', 'What did not go as planned?', 'What can I do to improve in future?'.

Although this book has concentrated largely on identifying our problems and techniques for solving them, it also pays to be aware of our time management strengths.

Sunday: self-assessment
Sunday was self-assessment day. We looked at setting up a time log and tackling some of our troublesome timewasters. In future we should:

- Compile a time log once every three to six months and compare it with previous time logs in our time management notebook. Have we improved? Is there a better structure to our days?
- Revisit the list of top 10 timewasters to identify the areas we need to work on
- Choose one bad habit that we want to change every week.
- Enlist the help of others where possible in changing our habits

Monday: mastering paperwork

On Monday, we faced up to our paperwork problems. If the desk is still piled high with paperwork, there is more work to be done in this area.

- Eliminate unnecessary paperwork. We should constantly review the paperwork arriving on the desk and put a stop to the low pay-off items
- Use the Raft technique: Refer it, Act on it, File it or Throw it away
- The measles test should be tried every few weeks to get us into the habit of dealing with paperwork the first time we see it
- Our files should be purged regularly to keep our information down to a manageable level.
- If we have difficulty retrieving documents, we need to re-evaluate our classification systems

Tuesday: planning

On Tuesday, we got to grips with planning. We set long-term business and personal goals, translated them into action plans, and finally looked at compiling to-do lists. From now on we need to:

- Review our goals continuously: What goals have we achieved? What new goals do we need to set?
- Alter our action plans to take advantage of changes in our circumstances
- Set aside a few minutes each day to follow the step-by-step process below for daily planning

1 Set aside five minutes for planning at the end of the day
2 Carry forward unfinished activities
3 Plan tomorrow's activities
4 Include goal-linked activities
5 Prioritise activities on the list
6 Delegate things to do where appropriate
7 Estimate time required for each task
8 After opening mail, make additions to list

Wednesday: managing meetings

On Wednesday, we looked at managing meetings. Before any future meetings we should ask ourselves, 'Is this meeting really necessary; what are the alternatives?'.

- Before meetings, we should be clear about the objectives we wish to achieve
- During meetings, we should ensure that the conversation is focused on achieving those objectives
- If there is no follow-up on decision/action points discussed during meetings, we have wasted our time

Thursday: projects

On Thursday, we turned our attention to projects and looked at the three phases leading to their successful completion.

- If we plan our projects carefully we are greatly increasing their chances of success
- Controlling the project is especially difficult when we are busy with a large number of other projects. To prevent important tasks slipping through the cracks we need to use our to-do lists. Project-related tasks should always be assigned an 'A' priority
- During the evaluation phase, we should identify the problems and successes that will help in managing future projects

Friday: taming the telephone

The telephone is one of the most useful management tools we have but at the same time the most dangerous.

- Incoming calls provide the greatest threat. Junk calls need to be kept to a minimum by screening and developing techniques for being brief
- Outgoing calls should be treated in the same way as meetings. What do we want to say? How did the other person respond? What points require follow up?

The next stage

If you have benefited from this book, the next stage is to organise your own company or departmental Office Productivity Week. Copies of this book should be distributed to everyone taking part so that you can work together with your colleagues to improve your time management skills. If everyone around you is working towards the same goal, the change should be dramatic and permanent. An organisation's culture can only change if its individual members are involved in, and committed to, that change.

If you have any comments on the book or wish to organise an Office Productivity Week please contact:

Declan Treacy
The Clear Your Desk! Organisation
5 Grove Footpath
Surbiton
Surrey
KT5 8AT

Tel: 081 399 4080